WINNERS ALL

CO-OPERATIVE GAMES FOR ALL AGES

published by
Pax Christi, 9 Henry Road, London N4 2LH
Tel: 01-800 4612

PAX CHRISTI wishes to thank the Nonviolence and Children Program, Friends Peace Committee, 1515 Cherry St., Philadelphia, Pa 19102, U.S.A., for permission to reproduce this material, much of which comes from their publications *For the Fun of it* and *A Manual on Nonviolence and Children.*

© Philadelphia yearly meeting of the
Religious Society of Friends Peace Committee.
Illustrations drawn by Ann Clark.
Printed by THE STANHOPE PRESS,
103 Hampstead Road, London NW1. Tel: 01-387 0041.

First published by Pax Christi UK in 1980.
Reprinted 1982, 1983, 1984, 1985, 1986, 1987, 1988, 1989.

ISBN 0 9506757 1 7.

INTRODUCTION

Some thoughts about games in general
Games are really important. They are an opportunity to build a sense of community and trust within the classroom, family or any social gathering. Children joyfully play games — inside and outside — with energy, laughter and seriousness. What may seem like frivolous and carefree behaviour is the children's way of learning about themselves, their environment and other people. As one of our psychologists put it:
"Children do not play because they are young. They are young in order to **play**."

Problems with games
Sometimes games are used thoughtlessly. An example is the stunt or trick used to break the ice; it is fun for everyone at the expense of one person. Elimination games are really only "fun" for the co-ordinated and fast players. The slow or awkward person, who is always "out" on the first round, is bound to accumulate "bad" experiences and may stop playing altogether.

Competition
In our culture winning is a valued commodity. In this society, competition tends to create barriers between people; thus everyone loses. Insensitive use of games, with high overtones of competition, can be harmful to the group as well as to the individual. Undoubtedly competition in itself has its beneficial side. It helps children to develop skills and measure themselves against the previous scores made. Still, hard work is needed by teachers, leaders or organisers to counteract the deeply ingrained reactions to winning or losing. Generally when someone

(or a team) wins, the smiling, congratulating attention is focused on that person (or team). The loser is expected to be a "good sport", or is kindly told "better luck next time". When recognition and self-respect are so closely connected to winning, no one wants to lose. The winner feels good; the loser may feel many things — angry, determined to win the next time at any cost, bitterly disappointed, not valued as a person. Children, and adults too, need to be appreciated for just who they are. When children are not feeling particularly valued by those around them, they are all the more likely to be crushed by losing and less likely to be supportive members of the classroom.

Use of co-operative games
Recognising that these competitive elements exist, these games can be used to focus on establishing rapport and good spirit among children or adults. Along with much affirming and becoming acquainted with individuals, co-operative games can be used to build up a feeling of support and caring in a group. These games have been selected in an attempt to ensure that no one is left out or is forced to compete against others or participate unequally.

Adults can play too
We need to play as much as children do. We do not have the natural energy — releasing connections to each other that children do — and may, therefore, have more need of playful activities. There may be resistance to initiating a

game because of our Western inhibitions: it's silly, foolish and a waste of time! However, hundreds of adults have played these co-operative games, among themselves, in a variety of situations and have enjoyed them tremendously. Adult participation in such games can lead to thoughtful discussion on attitudes towards values such as competition and success. The games could be used in many of the groups of which we form part — work, church, committees, parent associations and so on.
They draw participants together through laughter, and diminish competition, with the result that people become more relaxed and open with each other and better able to work as a unit: everybody wins.

A POSTER CHOICE
An "Introduction" activity.
This is a very useful exercise for helping people to feel confident. Confident to express their opinions. It is particularly useful at the beginning of a course or conference. First, it is necessary to have a display of some kind — posters or cartoons are very suitable. Each person selects three items from the display — the most interesting, the most striking, the most relevant — or whatever criteria the leader suggests. This initial **personal** choice is very important for what ensues.
The next stage is for each participant to find a partner. The two then explain their choices to each other, and then, as a pair, have to do the exercise again. That is to get three items between the two of them. Then each **pair** meets up with another **pair** and the whole process is repeated once more. The final stage involves simply trying to identify which three or so items in the whole display have received most "votes" from the group as a whole.
There are all sorts of variations on this theme, but it is worth always keeping the basic format, i.e.:
First — individual choice.
Second — people talking in pairs.
Third — people talking in fours.

GESTURE NAME GAME
This game is a very physically active one which, as well as being lively fun, is a good way of introducing people to each other for the first time. The players should form a circle and each person in turn, without thinking, should make a gesture while saying his/her name at the same time. Name and gesture should go together in some sort of rhythm — for example, Bob Jacobs raises his hand while saying Bob and stamps one foot on the first syllable of Jacobs and his other foot on the second syllable. Then the entire group repeat together the name and the gesture. Thus all the group says everybody's name in a very lively way.

QUALITY INITIALS
To start a group meeting positively, each person thinks about two or three initials of her/his name (e.g. Chris Grant would take "C" and "G") and finds two **affirming** qualities that describe himself/herself (in Chris' case "cheerful and generous"). The attractiveness of this activity is that it gives people a chance to think about themselves in an affirming way.

SUE'S GAME
Everyone takes a paper and pencil and fills in the blanks in these sentences and signs his/her name.
If I were a colour, I'd be ....
If I were an animal, I'd be ....
If I were a fabric, I'd be ....
If I were an athlete, I'd be ....
If I were an actor/actress, I'd be ....
What others can you think of?

The group leader then collects the papers and reads them anonymously, having people guess who wrote them.

MEETINGS

Music needed; any number of players; large space. When the music starts, players walk around quickly in all directions, avoiding contact. When the music stops, each player shakes hands with the nearest person and discovers as much personal information as possible until the music restarts (5-7 seconds). The process is repeated; each time the player must greet someone new. The game continues until all have met.

Note: — Keep moving.

BUMP

For this game a large space is needed with music of some kind. It is suitable for any number of players. When the music starts all players walk round in all directions, deliberately bumping **gently** into as many others as possible. When the music stops each player stops and links arms with his/her nearest neighbour, exchanging names. When the music starts again, the players should remain in linked pairs and continue to walk around the room, this time avoiding bumps and continuing to talk to their partners. The music stops again and the pairs separate. Each player now grabs **two** other people who link arms and introduce themselves. The music starts again and the groups walk around and talk until the music stops. From now on, each time the music stops, the leader calls a different number and the groups form and re-form accordingly. When the leader feels that everyone has met everyone else, he or she

can start making the groups bigger and bigger until, perhaps, the whole is one large group linked noisily together!
Variation:–
With young children, simply use the music's stopping as the time to give a new instruction, e.g. walk around shaking players' hands; hugging them; walking backwards; touching elbows etc etc.

CHOOSING TEAMS CO-OPERATIVELY
The teacher/leader picks two Captains, each of whom picks one team member. Each member in turn chooses someone else, and so on down the line. In this way each team member will have the opportunity to choose someone — except for the last player chosen.

Though this method does not eliminate "the last choice" embarrassment, usually there is a different "last person" each time.

MAGIC MICROPHONE
This is a group co-operation technique that facilitates large group discussions. Choose an object (a can, book, block of wood, etc.) that is large enough to see and light enough to pass around. This object becomes the magic microphone. When one person has it, it is that person's special time to talk. Co-operation occurs when the microphone is shared. It is important to treat the microphone with respect.

JUMP-IN EXERCISE
Ask participants to jump into a circle in a way that they think expresses themselves. Afterwards, ask how people felt doing this. If people jump in individually, the exercise is affirming to the person, whereas if everyone jumps in together, it is more of a group-building exercise.

DRAGON
This game works best with either seven adults/not more than seven or eight children.
Everyone gets into line holding the waist of the person

in front, with their **hands** — not arms. Then the "head" i.e. the first person in the line of the dragon tries to touch the "tail" i.e. the last person in line, while the "body" i.e. the people in between, help to keep the "tail" from being touched, without anyone losing grip of the waist of the person in front.

If there is more than one line, then each line can operate independently of each other **or** think up something which would cause the various lines to interact.

NON-VERBAL BIRTHDAY LINE-UP
The leader gives only these instructions:— "Without talking, line yourselves up according to the month of your birth and possibly even the day and date." The players themselves must work out the beginning, end and order of the line, by mime or any other non-verbal communication.

TOUCH BLUE

The leader announces, "Everyone touch blue" (or another colour, object etc.). Participants must touch something on another person. "Touch a sandal" or "Touch a bracelet" ensures physical contact. Endless variations are possible e.g. Touch a left ear with your right thumb. Some teachers of young children find it interesting to allow children to play this game in "slow motion". Some children enjoy moving ver-r-ry slowly!

MUSICAL LAPS

This is a co-operative version of Musical Chairs. Players stand in a circle, close together, all facing in one direction, each with hands on the waist of the player ahead. When the music starts, everyone begins to walk slowly forward. When the music stops everyone sits in the lap of the player behind him or her. If the whole group succeeds in sitting in laps without anyone falling to the floor, the **group** wins. If players fall down, **gravity** wins. This game works best with more than ten players of about the same size.

Note: If players are co-operating, the circle will stay up and everyone will have a comfortable lap to sit on. If people do not sit gently or help others to find a seat, then the circle falls down.

SARDINES

One person hides. After a suitable interval, the rest go to find the "hider". When someone finds the hider, he or she hides alongside and keeps quiet until everyone is hiding in the same place. The first finder becomes hider next time. More fun if played in the dark.

PRU-EE
A delightful activity for large groups (fifteen or more). All eyes should be closed. The leader whispers in someone's ear, "You're the PRU-EE". Now everyone, including the Pru-ee, begins to mingle with eyes shut. Each person is to find another's hand, shake it and ask, "PRU-EE?" If the other person also asks, "PRU-EE?" they drop hands and go on to someone else. Everyone goes round asking except the PRU-EE, who remains silent the whole time. When a person gets no response to the question, "PRU-EE?" he or she knows the PRU-EE is found and hangs on to that hand, and becomes part of the PRU-EE, also remaining silent. Anyone else shaking hands with the PRU-EE (now two people) becomes part of it, making it larger and larger. If someone finds only clasped hands and silence, he or she can join the line at that point.

Soon the cries of PRU-EE will dwindle, and the PRU-EE will increase until everyone in the room is holding hands. Then the leader asks for eyes to be opened. There are usually gasps of surprise and laughter.

NOTE: The "PRU-EE?" sounds like a high-pitched little bird-call.

VEGETABLE CART
People sit in a circle with one person in the centre. People, by pairs, choose a vegetable. Centre player calls the names of one or more vegetables. Those players whose vegetables are called must get up and switch chairs while centre player tries to grab one of the two vacant chairs. The player who failed to get a chair becomes centre player and the game continues. If centre player calls "Vegetable Cart" then everyone changes seats.
With twenty or more people, each group of four is **one** vegetable.
Caution: Strong sturdy chairs — and lots of room — are needed.
Variation: Some familiar variations of this game, use names of important towns and have train service between them or letter delivery e.g. the 8.40 travelling from London to Liverpool; letters from Bath to Bristol etc etc.
"All stations change"/"General Post". This also gets entire group "on the move".

LET'S BUILD A MACHINE
People try to represent a "machine" with each person portraying a moving part. The "machine" can be imaginary, allowing scope for creativity in the "wheres" and "hows" of moving parts. Or it can be a real machine (washing, sewing or "school" machine theme) in which the fun lies in trying to figure out how to represent the parts with people. This game is good in the physical contact as well as the co-operation category.
NOTE: "Machine" Game is good for the physically handicapped, who can use crutches etc. A person confined to a wheelchair can be of central importance.

RAINSTORM
One person acts as the conductor of the storm and stands in the centre of a circle of players. As with an orchestra, the conductor brings each person into the storm (symphony) in turn. Standing in front of the first person, the conductor starts rubbing his/her hands together, copied

by the first person. Then the conductor turns slowly round on the spot to each person in turn until they are all performing the action which sounds like gentle, and increasingly heavy, rainfall. The conductor then repeats the whole process with a new action — snapping fingers, hands slapping thighs, stamping feet — which makes the sound of the crescendo of the storm. As with a sudden thunder shower, the conductor decreases the volume by going through the above steps in reverse until the last person rubbing hands is silent.

I LOVE YOU HONEY BUT I JUST CAN'T SMILE
Participants sit in a circle for this laughter-producing "Light and Lively". Begin by saying to the person to your right or left: "Do you love me honey?" That person responds: "Yes, I love you honey, but I just can't smile." The first person then attempts to make the second person smile. This continues around the circle until the first person is asked: "Do you love me honey?" and is made to smile.

MAGIC BOX
This is a "pantomime game"
Place an imaginary MAGIC BOX in the centre of the circle of players. Each player, in turn, goes to the box and "takes out" something and at the same time mimes an activity connected with the imaginary object he/she has taken out.

For example a player could take out a racquet and mime a tennis game.

When others in the circle have guessed the mime, and the accompanying object or objects, they may go to the centre of the circle and join in. No words are spoken. The originator then tells the others if they have guessed the object(s) correctly.

They all return to their places, in the circle, and another player "takes" something out of the box. The game continues until all have had a turn.

LAP BALL

All the players sit on the floor in a circle with their legs extended in front of them and so that everybody's feet are in the centre. The players' hands support their bodies by being placed behind the bodies on the floor. Heels are not to be lifted and hands must stay behind the back, although they can move. The object of the game is to keep the ball off the ground, while passing it quickly from lap to lap. If it gets stuck around the ankles, the group must think up some way of getting it moving again. The fun increases when two balls are being passed simultaneously in different directions. The co-operative challenge of the game is evident when two players are working together to keep the ball from falling between them onto the floor.

SINGING SYLLABLE

All sit in a circle. One person goes out of the room. The rest of the group picks one word with three or more syllables, e.g. No-vem-ber. Count off by syllables so that each player has a syllable. Then choose a simple tune, such as "Row, row, row your boat . . ." Each player sings his/her syllable to the tune of the song. For example, one would sing "no, no, no," etc. and another person would sing "vem, vem, vem" etc., to the same tune, and so on. Then the person who volunteered to go out of the room returns and tries to put the different syllables together and identify the word.

HUMAN PRETZEL

Two people leave the room. The others hold hands in a circle and twist themselves over and under and through each other without dropping hands. The two people waiting outside come back in and are challenged to untangle the group. The Pretzel co-operates as the "untanglers" figure out who goes where.

KNOTS

This is a variation of the Pretzel game.
Everyone closes eyes and moves together, each person taking another person's hand in each of his or her hands. When each person has two hands, then all open their eyes and try to untangle themselves without dropping hands. The group must work together to get out the knots. It leads to very amusing situations because, although the group may end up in one big circle, most of the time there will be a knot or two in the circle, and even two or more circles, either intertwined or separate. It leads to group co-operation.

BLIND NEIGHBOUR
This works best if people know each other well. Chairs in a circle, one for each person. Half of the group sits down, with alternating vacant chairs. They shut their eyes. The other people then take the vacant chairs and start singing, perhaps each singing a different song. Each shut-eyed person tries to guess who is sitting to the right. If the singing together makes it too difficult for the shut-eyed people to guess then the open-eyed people should sing one at a time. After the guessing, reverse roles and start again.

ZOOM
This is a large group circle game which encourages laughter. Imagine "Zoom" as the sound of a racing car. Start by saying "Zoom" and turning your head to either side of the circle. The person on that side passes the word "Zoom" to the next person, and so on until everyone has quickly passed "Zoom" around the circle. Next, explain that the word "Eek" makes the car stop and reverse direction. Thus, whenever the word "Eek" is said, the "Zoom" goes the opposite way around the circle. At first, it may be helpful to allow only one "Eek" per person per game thus preventing the "Eeks" and "Zooms" from being concentrated in one area of the circle. Later, this might be

used as a co-operation game by avoiding the rule but letting each participant feel a responsibility for helping to balance "Eeks" in different segments of the circle and to thus help the "Zoom" to get all the way around. If the group isn't too large, it may be a good idea to continue the game until everyone has had a chance to say "Eek". If quite large, everyone who did not say "Eek" can be given a chance to "Eek" together.

CLAPPING GAME

One player leaves the room. The rest of the group decides upon an object for the person to find or an action for him/her to perform. The player outside is then brought in and tries to find his object or activity while the group claps. The group helps the player to complete the task by clapping louder and louder as the person approaches the object or act decided upon. If the person is far away from finding their objective, then the clapping becomes soft.

CANDY EAT

The players should divide into teams of three. One by one each team is allotted a piece of unwrapped hard toffee suspended by a string about twelve inches above the tallest person in the group. The group of three is then told that they can have the piece of candy if they can get it down without touching the string or candy with their hands. The only way to do this is for two of the group to lift the third who then gets the candy down with his/her teeth — they can then share the candy.

HERMAN HENRIETTA

Herman Henrietta is an imaginary blob of clay that can be shaped into anything. The leader/teacher begins to mime, pulling the imaginary blob from his/her pocket and sets the tone of the game by seriously beginning to create something. To start with it is a good idea to create something very simple that the children or players can easily identify. It is fun to guess the object but not necessary, as the object of the game is a quiet concentration on what another person is doing. After the leader has finished, the magical lump is pressed down to its original size and passed reverently to the next person. The game continues around the circle.

FARMYARD

The players stand in a large circle and choose a number of animals. For a group of twenty about six would be suitable. The animals should be divided as equally as possible among the group — each person having the name of his/her animal given on prepared pieces of paper. Then, with all the players' eyes closed (or if possible in a darkened room) the players should walk about and find their own kind by constantly calling out in the call of their own kind — "Baa-baa" — "Meow, meow" and so on. When two animals of one kind come across each other they should hold hands and find others of their kind until the group is complete.

Note: The idea is not to finish first, but merely to find others of your own kind.

ONE WORD STORY
Circle formation. Each person in turn says one word which will add to the story that is developing. For example "I . . . saw . . . a . . . monster . . . in . . . the . . . lemon . . . soup . . ." and so on. Very amusing. It works best when the pace is **lively.**

REFLECTIVE LISTENING STORY TELLING
Everyone is sitting in a circle. Someone starts a story. The teacher or leader sets the tone by starting with something he or she knows would catch the group's interest, stopping at some dramatic moment. The next person to left or right takes over the story. Encourage short and lively accounts.

ELEPHANT AND PALM TREE
Begin this game with everyone standing in a circle. One person stands in the middle and points to someone in the circle, saying "elephant!" or "palm tree!" To make an "elephant", the person pointed to leans over, clasping his/her hands and swinging his/her arms to form the "trunk". The person on his/her left makes the "elephant's left ear" by holding up his/her left elbow and touching the top of his/her head with his/her left hand. The person to the right of the "elephant trunk" does the same with his/her right arm to form the "elephant's right ear". To make the "palm tree", the person in the centre stands with hands straight up (the "trunk"). Those on each side hold up their outside arms, hands drooping, to make "fronds". It is fun for people to make up their own versions of this game.

RHYTHM CLAP
This is good for large groups (ten or more). Everyone closes eyes and begins to clap or beat any rhythm he or she chooses. At first, it will sound disjointed and chaotic, but gradually people try to change in order to create a fine rhythmical experience. It can end at any time by players opening eyes or by slowing down the rhythm. People who believe themselves to be without rhythm will feel pleased with the activity.

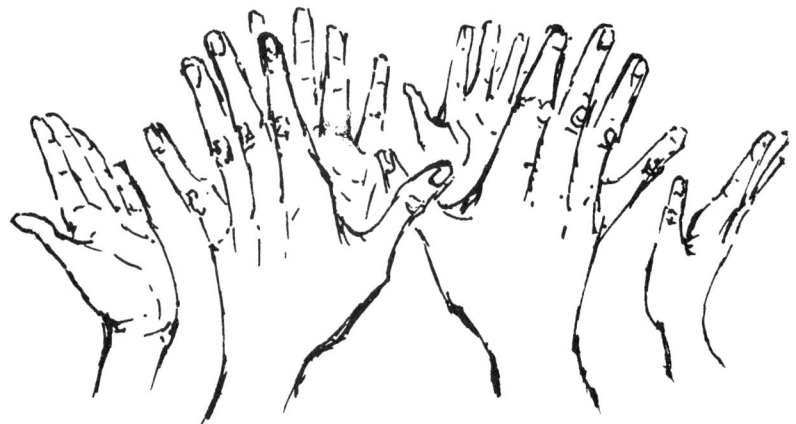

SWITCHBACKS
All the players should stand in pairs back to back. If there is an odd number of people, the free person can sing or talk in monologue, or play some simple kind of instrument such as a drum or tambourine, while everyone moves around the room back-to-back with their partner — it is a good idea to lock elbows. When the singing stops, each person must find a new partner. The current "odd" person is now the music maker and the game is repeated. If there is an even number of people, there is no free person and someone is chosen as caller (while participating).

Variations:— When music/singing ceases the caller can tell people to touch various parts of the body — stand head to head or toe to toe or, at a signal, to simply face partner and start a quiet conversation.

SLIP THE DISC
Everyone forms a circle, kneeling on hands and knees with heads facing inward. A light object, e.g. a four inch diameter circular piece of cork or a frisbee is placed upon one person's back. The object of the game is to pass the cork disc successfully from back to back around the circle without the use of hands. If it falls, it is replaced (by hands) on the back of the last person who had it.

PAN PONG
Each player has a pan (a saucepan, frying pan, dish pan or tray will do). The players form a circle. One player bounces the ball out of his/her pan into the next player's pan. The purpose of the game is to see how long the players can keep up bouncing the ball from one pan into the next one's pan. If players cannot get the ball on to the next pan in one bounce, they can keep bouncing the ball until the transfer can be made.

CO-OPERATIVE JUMPING ROPE
Two players turn a rope. The other players line up to jump. The first player jumps once, runs out and takes one end of the rope. The player he/she takes it from goes to the end of the line. Meanwhile the second player has to jump **twice,** run out and take the rope from the other player who has been turning it, relieving that player to go to the end of the line. The third player jumps three times and runs out, the next player four times and so on — each player taking alternate ends of the turning rope. If a "miss" occurs, the next player begins over again, jumping once, the next twice, and so on.

CENTRE THROW
Players form a circle, with one player standing in the centre. The centre player throws the ball to any player in the circle and immediately runs to any other player. That player then runs to the centre to receive the ball thrown by the player last receiving it. The game continues until all have been the centre player.

THROUGH THE LOOP

The players stand in a line, one behind the other with the first player facing all the others. There must be an odd number of players with seven as the ideal number. Player two, the first of the line facing player one should arch his/her arms over his/her head. Player three then throws the ball to player one through the arched arms of player two. A point is scored for the class if the throw is successful. Player one then moves swiftly to the near end of the seven, taking the ball to four on his/her way. Player four then moves to the position of three and throws the ball to player two (who is now in the position of one) through the arched arms of player three, and so the game continues. In a large class several groups of seven players will be needed. The total score is a class effort.

THREE DEEP

Players form a double circle, each player of the inner circle having someone stand immediately behind him/her. One player stands in the centre of the circle. The centre player throws a ball to someone in the inner ring. Immediately after releasing the ball, the centre player runs and stands behind the outer-player partner of the one to whom he/she has thrown the ball. The player who receives the ball — now one of a three-deep set — must then run to the centre and throw the ball to another inner player — running to the back of his/her set, and so the game continues.

ROUND ROBIN PING-PONG

This Ping Pong is played with two wooden bats (as in Table-Tennis), one at each end of the table. Players (at least five or six — preferably ten) are lined up on both sides. Two players from opposite sides, using the bats, begin by hitting the ball to one another. As soon as a player has hit the ball, he or she quickly places the bat on the table and runs to the end of the line. Meanwhile, the next player has picked up the bat and hits the ball, drops the bat and quickly moves out of the way of the next person. The ball should be hit **gently** and **slowly** until people are confident.

Participants initially should decide direction of the movement. After a while, people may want to move in the opposite direction. If so one of the "batsmen" shouts "Switch!" which signals everyone to reverse direction. Probably the two players "batting" should hit the ball several times to allow a few extra seconds for participants to switch direction.

WATER-CUP PASS

Everyone stands in a circle with a paper cup in his/her teeth. One person's cup is filled with water. That person begins by pouring water into the next person's cup without using hands and so on around the circle. A delightful game on a hot summer day.

CO-OPERATION SQUARES
A game with emphasis on group-functioning.
This game places participants in a conflict situation which cannot end until each group co-operates.
1. Before class prepare a set of squares for each group of five children. (A set consists of 5 envelopes containing pieces of stiff paper cut into patterns that will form five 6" x 6" squares as below).

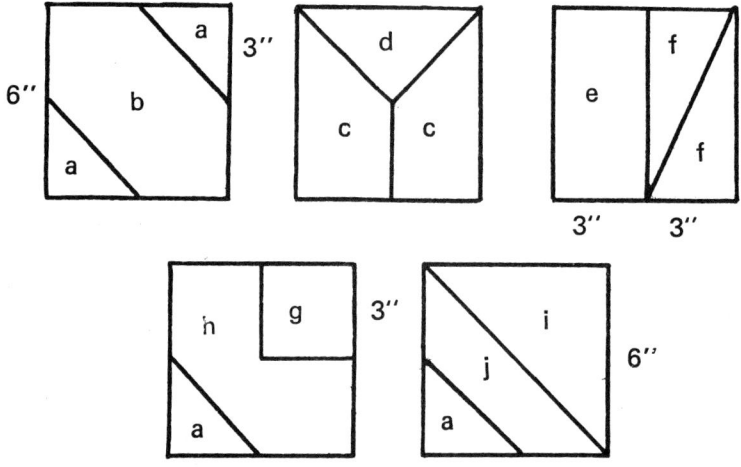

Several **individual** combinations will be possible but only **one total** combination.
2. Cut each square into parts a to j and lightly pencil in the letters. Then mark the envelopes A to E and distribute the pieces thus: envelope A — pieces a, c, h, i; envelope B — pieces a, a, a, e; envelope C — piece j only; envelope D — pieces d and f; envelope E — pieces b, c, f, g. Erase the small letters from the pieces and write instead the envelope letters A to E so that the pieces can be easily returned for re-use.

3. Divide the class into groups of five and seat each group at a table. Give each group member an envelope and ask that the envelope be opened only on a signal.
4. Describe the game as a puzzle involving conflict and co-operation. Read the instructions aloud and give the signal to open the envelopes. The instructions are as follows:

> Each person has an envelope containing pieces for forming squares. At the signal, the task of the group is to form five squares of equal size. The task is not completed until everyone has before him or her a perfect square, and all the squares are of the **same size.**
>
> During the game no member may speak. No member may communicate in any way — by smiles, hand-signals, longing glances etc. No member may **take** a puzzle piece from anyone else. Members may **give** puzzle pieces to others. Some class members should be observers. As groups finish allow them to observe other groups — silently.

It will usually take about 20 minutes for all groups to finish. You should spend at least as much time discussing the game as you spend playing it.

The following questions might be helpful in provoking discussion:
1. How did you feel?
2. How did the holder of envelope C feel?
3. Did anyone notice that C had only one piece?
4. How did you feel when someone held a piece and did not see the solution?
5. Why did you take all the pieces?
6. What was your reaction when someone finished a square and then sat back without seeing if that solution prevented others from solving the problem?
7. Were you afraid you would look foolish because you couldn't see a solution?
8. What were your feelings if you finished your square

and then began to realise you would have to break it up and give away a piece?
9. How did you feel about a person who did not follow directions?
10. How did you feel about a person who was slow at seeing the solution or who misunderstood the instructions?
11. What processes enabled some groups to finish quickly? Did you follow the instructions? If not, how do you feel? Satisfied? Angry?

Note: Obviously this game is geared to older children, but an enterprising teacher could adapt it for juniors.

Acknowledgement:

In its basic format, this exercise was first published in the N.E.A. Journal, U.S.A., October 1969.

SEQUENCE SETS

A card game suitable for children from four years. There may be three or four, or even five, players — more than five means that turns come round too infrequently.

Take forty blank cards, say half the size of a playing card. Divide into four sets of ten. On each set of ten write the numerals 0 to 9 in coloured felt pen, using a different colour for each set. Shuffle the forty cards.

The co-operative object of the game is to build up four colour sets (or piles) in sequence 0 to 9.
To play:—
Deal out the cards. For convenience each player sorts his/her cards into colour sets, face upwards for all to see, but in front of himself/herself. The first player places a zero in the centre. Before playing his/her turn, each player should look at his/her neighbour's cards so that he/she can, if possible, play down his/her own card so that his/her neighbour is able to follow with another card. Some children will be able to look further than their neighbour's card when they have a choice of what to play. The game continues until all four sets are complete. A player with several cards left may give a card or cards to a player who has used all his/her cards.

Trust games
These exercises help people to feel more positive about each other and they also promote better co-operation in a group. It is important that such games should only be used when groups have had a chance to grow together.

THE BLINDFOLD TRUST WALK
People divide into pairs. One person leads the other person blindfolded or with the eyes closed. The leader/teacher leads the blindfolded partner about and explains where he/she is taking him/her, what to expect, and re-assures him/her that he/she will not fall or bump into anything. The blindfolded partner should have complete trust in the

person leading. After a few minutes the partners switch roles. When everyone has had a chance to be blindfolded the participants get back together in a group and discuss how it felt to lead and be led.

THE TRUST FALL
This also builds community in a group and is also affirming to the one who is falling. Several people stand close together in a circle and hold out their hands. One person stands **inside** the circle, remaining fairly rigid. He/she then "falls" into the circle and is caught by the people closest to where he or she falls. The group must take great care not to allow the person to fall to the floor. Then the person who fell can be passed around the circle. If there is time everyone who wishes should get a chance to do the "trust fall".

For the very young
Co-operative games adapted for nursery and reception classes and for more informal playgroups etc.

KANGAROO HOP
This is an energetic tag game which is a lot of fun and excellent for letting off excess energy. One player is "it", or the tagger, and the first person who is tagged is the lucky one because he or she becomes a kangaroo and hops around trying to catch someone else. As soon as the next child is tagged he/she joins the first person in hopping round and tagging the others. In the end everyone is a hopping kangaroo.

PASS THE MASK
This is a very good game for young children as they do it very well. The group of children should sit in a circle and the first child makes a funny face — the next child (to the left or right) makes the same face as he/she is shown and then makes one of his/her own to the next child — who then repeats it back to him/her and then

makes one of his/her own. Thus each person in the circle has to imitate and invent a funny face.

ELECTRIC SQUEEZE
The children should stand in a circle holding hands. One child gently squeezes the hand to his/her left and that child squeezes the one to his/her left and so on. The idea is for the children to watch the electric squeeze being passed from person to person around the circle.

PASSING A HUG
The children should stand in a circle. One person starts by giving a hug to the child on his/her left and so on round the circle.

GOING FOR A WALK
Choose a leader. Sit in circle formation, up straight, hands palms downward on knees. "Walk" by beating palms on knees. The leader could demonstrate this before the game begins. The leader's directions should be clear and appropriate and well mimed. Except where another action is indicated "walking" is mimed. The children repeat "story words" and actions after the leader each time.

LEADER
Let's go for a walk.
We're coming to a river.
We can't go over it.
We **must** go **through** it. (Swimming action)

We're coming to a big tree.
We can't go around it.
We can't go through it.
We **must** go **over** it. (Climbing and sliding down)

We're coming to a mountain.
We can't go round it.
We can't go through it.
We **must** go **over** it .

We're coming to a big cave.
We can't go round it.
We can't go over it.
We **must** go **through** it.

THERE'S A MONSTER IN THE CAVE!

All "run" (fast walking mime) back to the beginning, repeating quickly in reverse all the phrases and mimes back to the beginning. The game can be repeated with a new leader.

AFFIRMATION CLAPPING

This is a birthday affirmation exercise which works well with younger children. One person is affirmed by everyone focusing their attention on him or her, and clapping where indicated, as follows:

Here is a clap for **(person's name)**
Here is a clap for health.
Here is a clap for wealth
And here is a clap for love upon you.
Here is a clap for all the years you've grown
And all you have to grow.

The verse can be followed by a burst of clapping affirming the individual.

A CLOSING CIRCLE

A closing circle is a short activity which draws the children at the end of a day or a play session to give a sense of closure. The teacher can link the game to something good that has happened during the day or, if the day has been a difficult one, choose an activity which provides a sense of community or uplift. Here are two suggestions:

i. Rhythmic clapping

This is a game that three to five year olds seem to love. When they first start, they clap wildly and without much rhythm, but with practice they get better and better, and achieve any rhythm set. if the leader needs the attention of the group, the activity can be ended by clapping very quietly which will make it possible to speak to the class.

ii. Catch a mouse

This is a game for those times when everyone needs a quiet break or a few moments to catch their breath. The teacher or leader should say to the children:— "Pretend that you are going to catch a mouse — you will need to walk very quietly to the rug (to your chairs etc. etc.) so that you will not scare the little animal." The children are thus challanged to see how quiet they can be.

Index of Games and Activities

A Closing Circle
Affirmation Clapping
A Poster Choice
Blind Neighbour
Bump
Candy Eat
Centre Throw
Choosing Teams Co-operatively
Clapping Game
Co-operation Squares
Co-operative Jumping Rope
Dragon
Electric Squeeze
Elephant and Palm Tree
Farmyard
Gesture Name Game
Going for a Walk
Herman Henrietta
Human Pretzel
I love you Honey but
    I just can't smile
Jump-in Exercise
Kangaroo Hop
Knots
Lap Ball
Let's build a machine
Magic Box
Magic Microphone
Meetings
Musical Laps
Non-Verbal Birthday Line-up
One Word Story
Pan Pong
Pass the Mask
Passing a Hug
Pru-ee
Quality Initials